Mimi & P. Pie Penelope May

Thank you from Allison

Thank you to my amazing husband, Tad, whose brilliant ideas, loving encouragement, and practical support have made this possible. Snuggles to my sweet P. Pie Penelope May for such fun and delightful inspiration. You are a treasure! Thank you to our dear daughter, Melissa, and our son-in-law-and-love, Shawn, for naming your children such fun names for these rhyming books! Thank you, Ellie, for bringing this to life so creatively and beautifully. And a huge thank you to the King and Creator of all for giving me such a precious family and incredible purpose in this season of life! I am truly beyond grateful!

Thank you from Ellie

My praise and thanks go to my Creator! A special thanks to you, Allison, for this incredible opportunity to collaborate on your wonderful story. Thank you to my husband, Clint, for encouraging me to be authentically me, for loving and helping me find time and space to illustrate. To my kiddos Tekoa, Avi, Happy, and Azzy – thank you for inspiring me and making me love being a mommy. Thank you, Patty, for believing in me. And to my sweetest friends at WG, thank you all for your encouragement to rise up and use the gifts God has given me to share with others!

Words by Allison Eley

ELEY PUBLISHING
AVA, MISSOURI

Art by Ellie Snyder

For my sons, my daughters, your amazing spouses,
all sixteen of my treasured grandchildren,
and any more that may be planned
in the heart of the
Heavenly Father.
Each of you is a
beautiful treasure!
May you tend the
garden of your heart
with care,
and may you encourage
each other with the
greatest flower of all...
LOVE.

Your Mama
and Mimi

P. Pie Penelope May!
Rise and shine, it's a beautiful day!

Hand in hand, they walk through the gate, to a lush green oasis where wonders await.

Nearby was a gold one named HOPE standing tall. Its petals like sunshine—a beacon to all. "Hope must grow strong, even in rain," Mimi explained, "through joy and through pain."

A short one named JOY,
Penelope spotted.
Its colors so vibrant,
its petals all dotted.

Joy is a treasure—a light in the night.
It makes the world sparkle, so happy and bright.

Another named PEACE—as they walked along—
was singing a calm, quiet masterpiece song.
"Peace is so gentle, so steady and kind."
Mimi said softly, "Shalom you will find."

PATIENCE and KINDNESS were there in a row.
HUMBLE and FAITHFUL, their fragrance you know
GOODNESS and GENTLENESS growing with care,
among SELF CONTROL ...

... all thriving with prayer.

The brightest of all, a flower named LOVE, reaching its face to the heavens above.

LOVE is the greatest, its beauty so pure.
God's gift to the world, the answer for sure!

Penelope looked at the flowers around,
each one a treasure, each one profound.

"Am I like these flowers?" she asked with a sway.

"Yes, my dear P. Pie Penelope May!"

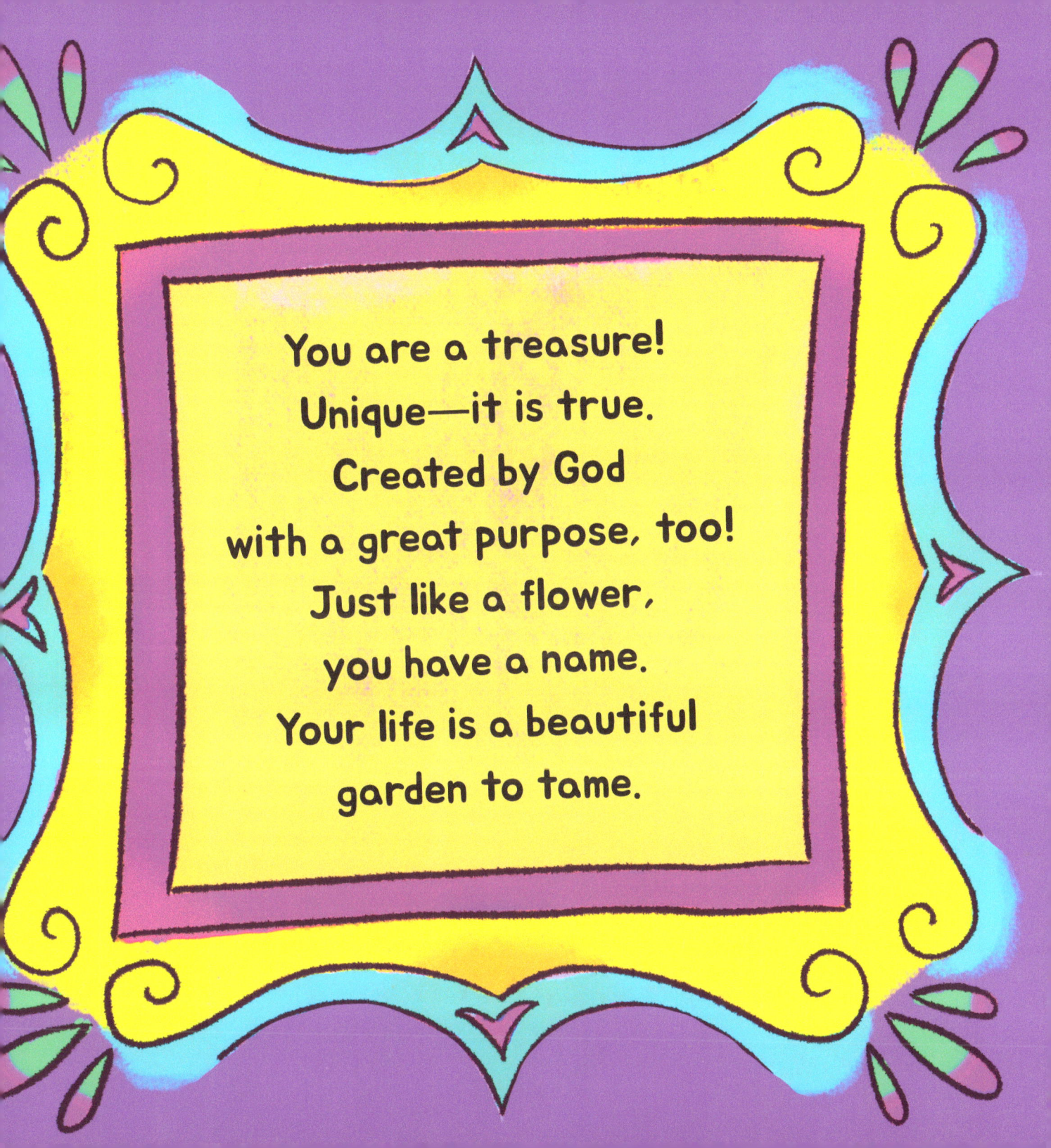

You are a treasure!
Unique—it is true.
Created by God
with a great purpose, too!
Just like a flower,
you have a name.
Your life is a beautiful
garden to tame.

To keep out the weeds,
we must choose the right seeds.
SELFISHNESS and PRIDE
lead to all the wrong deeds.

They choke out the beauty
and steal the sweet song.
In our life's garden,
the weeds don't belong.

Thank you, dear God,
for this wonderful day.

In your garden of love,
I want to stay.

Penelope beamed, feeling special inside—
knowing in God's love, she'd always abide.

With seeds in her pocket of flowers so sweet, planting her own garden will be such a treat.

We plant and we tend the garden with love,
God's perfect design for us from above.
We water—He grows these flowers so fair,
the choice is ours to tend them with care.

What are the seeds you're planting in you?

Your life is a garden that must be well-tended, the soil of your heart needs to be well-amended.

With lots of love and intentional care,
just like the flowers P. Pie saw there—
you have a name and a great purpose, too...

You are a treasure! Yes, it is true!

... a note from the author ...

One of the most important legacies we can pass on to our children is the character they carry.

This book is the first in a series designed to help children—and the grown-ups who love them—cultivate hearts that are kind, strong, tender, and rooted in truth. These stories aid in equipping them with the tools they need to face life's challenges with strength and grace.

P. Pie Penelope May learns how to recognize what's growing in the garden of her heart, and how to grow what's good while pulling what doesn't belong. These are not just children's stories—they are a roadmap for raising healthy individuals ... because the greatest gift we can pass on to our children is a well-tended heart. Through the journey of P. Pie Penelope May, readers of all ages are invited to tend the garden of their hearts: to plant virtues like patience, kindness, joy, and love, and to intentionally remove weeds like pride and selfishness. These are not just lessons for childhood. They are lifelong truths that shape how we live, love, and leave our legacy.

There will always be challenges along the journey. Our great responsibility and privilege is to equip our little ones with the character qualities necessary for walking victoriously through those challenges. While these truths are essentials that must be profoundly protected, and passed on to those who come after us, it takes a lifetime for us to collect the seeds and nurture them into strong, healthy, deeply rooted perennials in our own lives. No matter what age, we all need to pay careful attention to what is growing in the garden of our hearts. How can we tend our heart's garden so that our interactions with others leave a lasting impression of blessing, beauty, and peace? We must commit to a lifelong endeavor of intentionally and continually planting and nurturing the flowers we read about in this book. The condition of our heart influences every word we speak, every action we take, and every life we touch. May this story inspire deep introspection, meaningful growth, and a lifelong commitment to nurturing beauty and purpose from the inside out.
Let's grow together!

With love and joy,
Allison Eley

Consider, dear friend, before we depart ...
what can be found in the soil of your heart?

"... Plant the good seeds of righteousness,
and you will harvest a crop of love.
Plow up the hard ground of your hearts,
for now is the time to seek the Lord,
that he may come and shower
righteousness upon you."
Hosea 10:12

"Guard your heart above all else,
for it determines the course
of your life."
Proverbs 4:23

Author Allison Eley

The author is deeply rooted in her roles as a devoted wife, supportive mother of five amazing adult children, mother-in-law and love to each of their wonderfully chosen spouses, and adoring grandmother of sixteen precious grandchildren. Her greatest joy and purpose are in loving her family well and endeavoring to live this life with light and love. Her heart's deepest desire is to leave a legacy of love—a legacy that will nurture and strengthen her family and those around her in the Creator's beautiful and perfect design for life.

Illustrator Ellie Snyder

Ellie Snyder has a deep love for beauty. She hopes that her talent and creativity will inspire others to love life, notice the subtle and profound beauty around them, think deeply, and cultivate love for the Creator. She currently lives on a farm in the Ozarks with her husband, four children, and many animals. She treasures time spent in the garden, where she is surrounded by a diverse array of beauty that is full of energy and life! Please visit www.joyofthemaker.com to learn more about her and her family.

Books by Allison Eley

Little Learners—Big Creator

  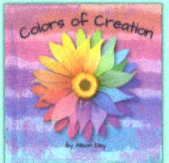   

Animal ABCs | Counting Fun with Fruits & Veggies | Colors of Creation | Patterns on Purpose | Original Opposites | The Creator's Design

Yahweh's Rhythms & Reminders

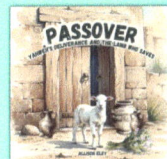  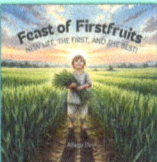  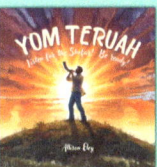 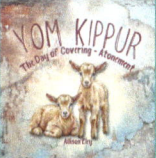 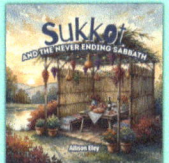

Passover | Feast of Unleavened Bread | Feast of Firstfruits | Shavuot | Yom Teruah | Yom Kippur | Sukkot

  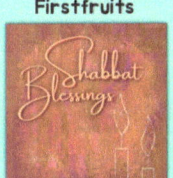 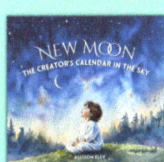 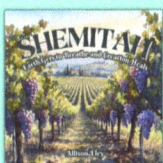  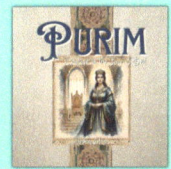

The King's Calendar | Little Reminders | Shabbat Blessings | New Moon | Shemitah | Hanukkah | Purim

P. Pie Penelope May

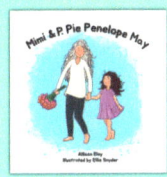

Mimi & P. Pie Penelope May

More to come in this series!

More books are blossoming! To enjoy the books already in bloom and see what is about to sprout, visit

eleypublishing.com

ELEY PUBLISHING

Every garden begins with a seed.
What will you grow today?

Text and layout © 2025 Allison Eley. All rights reserved. Printed in the United States of America. Scripture quotations are taken from the Holy Bible, New Living Translation, copyright © 1996, 2004, 2015 by Tyndale House Foundation. Used by permission of Tyndale House Publishers, Inc., Carol Stream, Illinois 60188. All rights reserved. No part of this book may be copied, stored, or shared in any form without written permission from the author, except for brief quotes used in reviews or educational settings. Illustrations were created by Ellie Snyder. For permission requests, contact Eley Publishing at eleypublishing@gmail.com, Ava, Missouri.
Library of Congress Control Number: 2025913063
Paperback ISBN: 978-1-967834-10-5
Hardcover ISBN: 978-1-967834-11-2

www.ingramcontent.com/pod-product-compliance
Lightning Source LLC
Chambersburg PA
CBHW041413010526
44107CB00016B/1159